GUINNESS WORLD RECORDS

GUINNESS WORLD RECORDS™

ULTIMATE
PET RECORDS

GUINNESS WORLD RECORDS

ULTIMATE PET RECORDS

Compiled by Kris Hirschmann and Ryan Herndon

For Guinness World Records:
Jennifer Gilmour, Laura Plunkett,
Craig Glenday, Stuart Claxton, Michael Whitty,
and Laura Nieberg

SCHOLASTIC INC.
New York Toronto London Auckland Sydney
Mexico City   New Delhi   Hong Kong

Guinness World Records Limited has a very thorough accreditation system for records verification. However, while every effort is made to ensure accuracy, Guinness World Records Limited cannot be held responsible for any errors contained in this work. Feedback from our readers on any point of accuracy is always welcomed.

© 2010 Guinness World Records Limited

No part of this work may be reproduced, stored in a retrieval system, or transmitted in any form or by any means, electronic, mechanical, photocopying, recording, or otherwise, without written permission of the publisher. For information regarding permission, write to Scholastic Inc., Attention: Permissions Department, 557 Broadway, New York, NY 10012.

Published by Scholastic Inc. SCHOLASTIC and associated logos are trademarks and/or registered trademarks of Scholastic Inc.

ISBN: 978-0-545-21021-8

Designed by Michelle Martinez
Photo Research by Els Rijper
Records from the Archives of Guinness World Records

12 11 10 9 8 7 6 5 4 3 2 1   10 11 12 13 14 15/0

Printed in the U.S.A.

First printing, January 2010

Visit Guinness World Records at www.guinnessworldrecords.com

CONTENTS

The idea for Guinness World Records grew out of a question. In 1951, Sir Hugh Beaver, the managing director of the Guinness Brewery, wanted to know which was the fastest game bird in Europe — the golden plover or the grouse? Some people argued that it was the grouse. Others claimed it was the plover. A book to settle the debate did not exist until Sir Hugh discovered the knowledgeable twin brothers Norris and Ross McWhirter, who lived in London.

Like their father and grandfather, the McWhirter twins loved information. They were kids when they started clipping interesting facts from newspapers and memorizing important dates in world history. As well as learning the names of every river, mountain range, and nation's capital, they knew the record for pole squatting (196 days in

1954), which language had only one irregular verb (Turkish), and that the grouse — flying at a timed speed of 43.5 miles per hour — is faster than the golden plover at 40.4 miles per hour.

Norris and Ross served in the Royal Navy during World War II, graduated from college, and launched their own fact-finding business called McWhirter Twins, Ltd. They were the perfect people to compile the book of records that Sir Hugh Beaver searched for yet could not find.

The first edition of *The Guinness Book of Records* was published on August 27, 1955, and since then has been published in 25 languages and more than 100 countries. In 2000, the book title changed to *Guinness World Records* and has set an incredible record of its own: Excluding non-copyrighted books such as the Bible and the Koran, *Guinness World Records* is the best-selling book of all time!

Today, the official Keeper of the Records keeps a careful eye on each Guinness World Record, compiling and verifying the greatest the world has to offer — from the fastest and the tallest to the slowest and the smallest, with everything in between.

INTRODUCTION

PET PARADE

For more than 50 years, Guinness World Records has measured, weighed, timed, verified, and documented the world's record-breakers in every category imaginable. Today, the records in their archives number more than 40,000.

This collection features 46 phenomenal pets on parade whose unique talents or extraordinary measurements earned them a Guinness World Record. Inside this book, we'll measure dog tongues and cat whiskers, jump guinea pigs, race ferrets, train service dogs, visit hospitals with horses, and chill out in the fanciest doghouse ever designed!

Whether your favorite pet has feathers or scales, wings or hooves, this is the ultimate book for animal lovers! Sit, stay, and get a treat by reading about the records set by these brave, smart, and furry friends of the family.

CHAPTER 1

Dog Days

People just *love* their pooches. They pamper them, teach them tricks, and show them off in every way imaginable from competitions to weddings. It's no wonder our archives are chock-full of canines and their tales of derring-do. In this chapter, you'll meet plenty of pups dubbed "Top Dog" thanks to some special talent or unique feature. We're going to the dogs . . . Guinness World Records style!

Largest Dog Wedding Ceremony

Record-holder:	"Bow Wow Vows"
Date:	May 19, 2007
Place:	Colorado, USA

The brides wore veils; the grooms wore bow ties; and *all* of the happy couples wore fur! "Howly" matrimony was the theme of the day at Bow Wow Vows, the **Largest Dog Wedding Ceremony** ever held (pictured). Organized by the Aspen Grove Lifestyle Center of Littleton, Colorado, this event united 178 pooch pairs on May 19, 2007. Some of the doggie duos had known each other for years. Others had met mere minutes earlier in a speed dating session. The ceremony had no legal status, but participants received a complimentary wedding "certificate" as a souvenir of their special day.

Doggie Play Dates

Dog owners like group activities, especially when setting a Guinness World Record. All dogs need to be taken for a walk and given a bath (pictured). Records can be broken when these chores are done with a group of friends! A year after organizing the **Largest Dog Walk**, Anthony Carlisle of the UK invited 2,506 *more* canines for a repeat outing on June 17, 2007. A record-breaking total 10,272 dogs participated in The Butcher's Great North Dog Walk in South Shields, Tyne and Wear, UK. How long would it take to bathe that many dogs? We'll have to keep wondering because the current record for **Most Dogs Washed** stands at 1,037 dogs bathed in eight hours by a team of 12 people in the Netherlands on June 6, 2008.

Largest Litter of Puppies

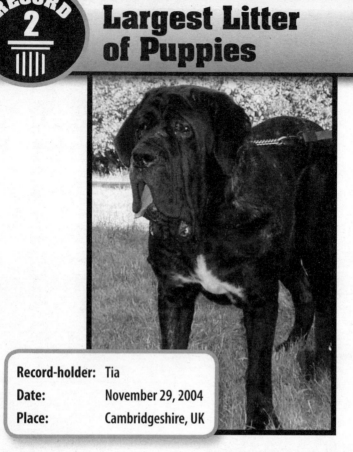

Record-holder:	Tia
Date:	November 29, 2004
Place:	Cambridgeshire, UK

Puppy love was in the air on November 29, 2004. On this momentous day, a Neapolitan Mastiff named Tia produced the **Largest Litter of Puppies** in history (pictured). Tia's brood totaled an astonishing 24 pups — 15 males and 9 females — but only 20 survived. Still there were too many puppies for Tia to handle. Owners Damian Ward and Anne Kellegher of Manea, Cambridgeshire, UK, helped Tia by bottle-feeding the hamster-size newborns for several weeks, until they were old enough to eat regular dog food.

Experts say that Neapolitan Mastiff pups should not be allowed to get too much exercise early on, because every scrap of energy is needed to nourish their growing bodies. A typical Neapolitan Mastiff gains over 100 pounds during its first year of life!

How big can a mastiff grow? Get the scales out for another record starring a relative of the Neapolitan Mastiff.

Tallest Dog

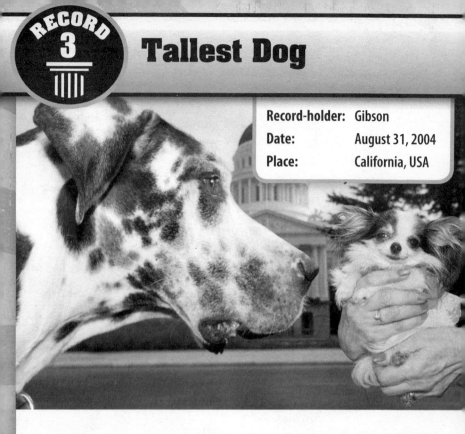

Record-holder:	Gibson
Date:	August 31, 2004
Place:	California, USA

A harlequin Great Dane named Milleniums' Rockydane Gibson Meistersinger was a true champion, in the record books and in life. Nicknamed "Gibson," the **Tallest Dog** measured 42.2 inches at the shoulder on August 31, 2004. Gibson had an important job as a therapy dog. He spent his days spreading cheer at hospitals, retirement homes, and schools. "He just puts a smile on people's faces," said owner Sandy Hall of Grass Valley, California. Pictured above, Gibson went nose-to-nose with Boo Boo, another record-holder at the opposite end of the ruler and on the next page, before his death on August 7, 2009.

Smallest Living Dog (Height)

Record-holder:	Boo Boo
Date:	May 12, 2007
Place:	Kentucky, USA

ULTIMATE FACTS

Lana loves to play dress-up with her petite pooch. "Boo Boo doesn't really care which clothes I put upon her tiny frame. [She is] the perfect candidate to model, and she doesn't mind wearing hand-me-down doll clothes," says Lana.

The world's **Smallest Living Dog (Height)** stands taller than a deck of standard playing cards — barely. A long-haired Chihuahua, Boo Boo measured exactly 4 inches at the shoulder when she was evaluated on May 12, 2007. She reached her current size around her first birthday, when she became eligible for Guinness World Records consideration. How small was Boo Boo at birth? No larger than a human thumb, the miniscule mutt weighed just an ounce and her owner, Lana Elswick of Raceland, Kentucky, had to hand-feed her every two hours with an *eyedropper* during the first few weeks of her life!

Smallest Living Dog (Length)

Record-holder:	Heaven Sent Brandy
Date:	January 31, 2005
Place:	Florida, USA

Hot dog! Yes, we're talking about an actual hot dog. That's about the length of Heaven Sent Brandy, a female Chihuahua who measures just 6 inches from the tip of her nose to the end of her tail (pictured). Called "Brandy" for short, this diminutive doggie has held the Guinness World Record for **Smallest Living Dog (Length)** since her official measurement on January 31, 2005. The two-pound pup lives in Largo, Florida, where she shares a kennel with her much-larger housemate, a boxer named Tyson. "They get on great," says owner Paulette Keller.

Small dogs need exercise, too. Paulette walks both of her different-sized pets at the same time. Pictured with Paulette is Tyson on the right and, look closely, Heaven Sent Brandy on the left.

Heaviest Dog Breed

Record-holder:	Old English Mastiff & Saint Bernard
Date:	1999
Place:	Worldwide

ULTIMATE FACTS

Mastiffs were originally trained to fight alongside soldiers during Roman times. Later this breed became a popular watchdog in England.

Saint Bernards were bred in Switzerland to help find travelers lost among the mountains during snowstorms.

These two dog breeds make terrific family pets, capable of loyalty and protectiveness for their family and home. But it's not a good idea to train them to be lap dogs! Regularly weighing between 170 and 200 pounds, adult male Old English Mastiffs and Saint Bernards share the Guinness World Record for **Heaviest Dog Breed** (pictured on this book's cover and to the right). These large dogs often outweigh their owners and could do a lot of damage, but are bred to be gentle and good-natured.

Plunge through this book's records to meet a heroic Saint Bernard named Barry.

Longest Dog Living

Record-holder:	Mon Ami von der Oelmühle
Date:	September 9, 2006
Place:	Wegberg-Arsbeck, Germany

See this couch-loving canine's family portrait in this book's special color-photo section.

ULTIMATE FACTS

Newborn Irish Wolfhounds weigh about one pound. But they grow up, and out, fast! Wolfhound puppies can add over an inch in height and 20 pounds in weight each month. By the end of its first year, an average wolfhound will stand about 30 inches tall and weigh about 100 pounds.

An Irish Wolfhound named Mon Ami von der Oelmühle doesn't quite meet the height requirements for a record, but he conquers all challengers in length at more than 7 ½ feet long! The proud holder of the Guinness World Record for **Longest Dog Living**, this incredible canine measures an astonishing 91.3 inches from nose to tail-tip. The record-breaker shares a home with owners Joachim and Elke Müller of Wegberg-Arsbeck, Germany. His nickname of "Monty" is about the *only* short thing when it comes to this prodigious pup!

Longest Tongue (Dog)

Record-holder:	Brandy
Date:	2002
Place:	Michigan, USA

If you held a long-tongue contest, a dog named Brandy would really "lick" the competition! Owned by John Scheid of St. Clair Shores, Michigan, this friendly boxer's tongue grew to 17 inches long — the **Longest Tongue (Dog)** ever recorded (pictured). Much too large to fit inside Brandy's mouth, this jaw-dropping organ was great for catching a drink or snatching some food from far away, and for attracting fame. At the peak of her popularity, Brandy had her own website and fan club. She also appeared on several TV shows before her death in 2002.

Oldest Dog Living

Record-holder:	Chanel
Date:	August 2, 2008
Place:	New York, USA

If you go by the classic formula, Chanel is 147 in human years. But old age hasn't stopped this wire-haired Dachshund female from enjoying every minute of her pampered life! Born on May 6, 1988, Chanel holds the Guinness World Record as the **Oldest Dog Living** (pictured). She enjoyed her 21st birthday party when this book went to press. Owners Karl and Denice Shaughnessy of Port Jefferson Station, New York, give Chanel all the respect due older generations. Explains Karl, "You treat her like you would treat your grandmother." The Shaughnessys give Chanel a special diet, a warm sweater, and goggles since their dog, like some older humans, has problems with her eyesight.

CHAPTER 2

Cat Tales

People have been fascinated by the mysterious feline species since the days of the ancient Egyptians. Now we've opened up the archives of Guinness World Records to find some record-breakers who are definitely the cat's meow! These kitties are eager to yowl about their fame and fortune, from an itty-bitty kitty that could curl up in a cup to the wealthiest cat in the world. These tales with tails will have you purring in amazement.

Largest Litter of Kittens

Record-holder:	Tarawood Antigone
Date:	August 7, 1970
Place:	Oxfordshire, UK

ULTIMATE FACTS

The gestation period (length of pregnancy) for cats is about 9 weeks. Most litters include between two and five kittens. It is rare for litters to produce more than eight kittens.

One mom raises 14 boys and a girl! Sounds like a TV comedy, right? We're talking about felines, not humans. These are the real-life stats for the **Largest Litter of Kittens** ever produced! The proud mother of this record-breaking litter was a 4-year-old Burmese/Siamese cat named Tarawood Antigone, owned by Valerie Gane of Kingham, Oxfordshire. The full litter, which was delivered by Cesarean section on August 7, 1970, consisted of 19 kittens. Four of the babies didn't make it. The other 15 survived to overwhelm their mother, overrun their owner's home, and outdo the other record contenders.

Cat with the Most Toes

Record-holder:	Jake
Date:	September 24, 2002
Place:	Ontario, Canada

Most cats have five toes on each front paw and four on each rear paw. That's a total of 18 toes for your average kitty. Jake, a cat owned by Michelle and Paul Contant of Bonfield, Ontario, Canada, is anything but average! This toe-riffic tabby has seven tootsies on each paw. Yes, that's 28 toes in total — more than enough to earn the Guinness World Record for **Cat with the Most Toes** (pictured). Jake's vet confirmed the count on September 24, 2002, after checking that *all* of his patient's piggies were "complete and distinct toes with normal nails, foot pads, and bone structure."

Longest Cat Whiskers

Record-holder:	Missi
Date:	December 22, 2005
Place:	Iisvesi, Finland

See Missi's magnificent whiskers up close in this book's special color-photo section.

ULTIMATE FACTS

The proper name for cats' whiskers is *vibrissae*. Cats have whiskers on the backs of their forelegs as well as on their faces.

Most cats use their facial whiskers to help them communicate their feelings and find their way around. But Missi, a Maine coon cat living in Iisvesi, Finland, with her owner Kaija Kyllonen, found a better use for her bristles. She used them to swipe the Guinness World Record for **Longest Cat Whiskers** away from the previous record-holder! Formally known as "Fullmoon's Miss American Pie," Missi earned her title on December 22, 2005, after official measurements confirmed that one of her whiskers was an amazing 7.5 inches long.

Longest Tail on a Domestic Cat

Record-holder:	Furball
Date:	March 21, 2001
Place:	Michigan, USA

ULTIMATE FACTS

Cats use tail position to communicate their feelings. An upright tail, for example, often means a cat feels happy or friendly. A twitching tail-tip shows annoyance, and a bristling tail shows anger or aggression.

The average male domestic cat has an 11-inch-long tail. Females' tails tend to be shorter — about 9.5 inches on average. No one told Furball about this fact, because she grew the **Longest Tail on a Domestic Cat** at an incredible 16 inches in length (nearly equal to Brandy the dog's famous tongue!). Owned by Jan Acker of Battle Creek, Michigan, Furball qualified for her Guinness World Record on March 21, 2001, after measurements were taken by a veterinary professional.

Longest Domestic Cat

Record-holder:	Leo
Date:	March 10, 2002
Place:	Illinois, USA

ULTIMATE FACTS

The Maine coon is a large cat breed, often weighing as much as 22 pounds. Leo, however, tips the scales at a magnificent 35 pounds. Leo's vet stresses that his patient is not fat. "His frame is big enough to carry this much weight," he says.

The **Longest Domestic Cat** has an extra-long name, just like his canine counterpart! Verismo's Leonetti Reserve Red, or "Leo" for short, is a Maine coon cat who measured a Guinness World Record-worthy 48 inches from nose to tail-tip on March 10, 2002 (pictured). That's about the height of an average 8-year-old human child. Owners Frieda Ireland and Carroll Damron of Chicago, Illinois, keep a careful eye on their pet whenever they're cooking. "He can stand up and put his paws on the kitchen counter," Frieda explains. Leo's massive paws could fit into size-2 kids' shoes!

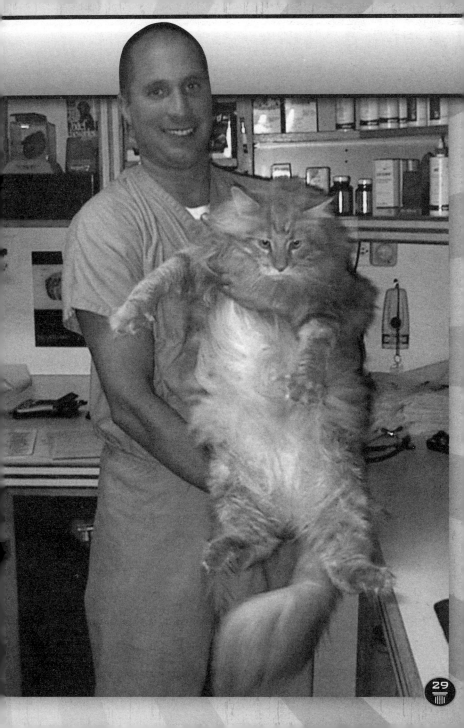

Smallest Living Domestic Cat

Record-holder:	Itse Bitse
Date:	November 24, 2003
Place:	Louisiana, USA

Itse Bitse is the perfect name for the **Smallest Living Domestic Cat** (pictured). Standing just 3.75 inches at the shoulder and measuring 15 inches from nose to tail-tip, this Himalayan/Siamese mix really is itsy-bitsy! Why so small? Itse Bitse is a munchkin, a specialized cat breed with legs much shorter than those of most cats. Owned by Mayo and Dea Whitton of West Monroe, Louisiana, Itse Bitse was fully grown when measured on November 24, 2003. Since that time, no other cat has been able to rise — or in this case, shrink — to the challenge of conquering Itse Bitse's Guinness World Record title.

Munchkin cats have a genetic disorder called achondroplasia, which is the same problem that causes dwarfism in humans. Shortened limbs are the main symptom of this disorder.

Double Threat

Technically, Itse Bitse doesn't hold just one Guinness World Record. She has actually earned two: the records for **Smallest Living Cat (Length)** and **Smallest Living Cat (Height)**. In many cases, these records belong to two different animals. This is the case with the world's smallest dogs. (See Boo Boo and Heaven Sent Brandy on pages 15 and 16.) Itse Bitse, however, is the tiniest cat in both respects, making her the all-around wee winner of the feline world.

Wealthiest Cat

Record-holder:	Blackie
Date:	May 1988
Place:	Buckinghamshire, UK

ULTIMATE FACTS

In his will, Ben Rea also left money to three cat charities, and to his gardener, plumber, car mechanic, and accountant. He left nothing to his human relatives.

Friends said that Ben Rea of Taplow, Buckinghamshire, UK, liked cats better than people. So perhaps it is not surprising that Ben, a retired antiques dealer who made millions investing in real estate, left the bulk of his fortune to his beloved cat, Blackie. The lucky kitty received $21.6 million upon his owner's death in May 1988, making him the **Wealthiest Cat** in history. What would a cat do with all that money? Blackie needs every one of his fabled nine lives to go through *this* incredible inheritance!

CHAPTER 3

Birds, Bunnies, and Buddies

Dogs and cats are the most popular pet species in the world today, but they aren't the only animals with star quality. Plenty of other pets have what it takes to become a record-holder . . . and this chapter proves it! You'll squawk with the chattiest birds, lift (*ooof*) big bunnies, find out what it takes to become a therapeutic pet, and much more. Are you ready to walk and talk with the animals?

Most Intelligent Parrot

Record-holder:	Alex
Date:	February 1999
Place:	Massachusetts, USA

See Alex counting in this book's special color-photo section.

Experts consider the African Grey parrot to be one of the world's smartest bird species. One special bird named Alex was at the head of the flock. The **Most Intelligent Parrot** was a resident of the Pepperberg Lab at Brandeis University in Waltham, Massachusetts. Dr. Irene Pepperberg worked closely with Alex for almost 30 years in studying and comparing intelligence among animal species (pictured). Alex could use more than 100 English words properly and count up to the number six. He was learning to read when he passed away on September 6, 2007. Irene's book, *Alex & Me*, details their lifetime spent learning about each other.

Oldest Cockatiel

Record-holder:	Pretty Boy
Date:	November 3, 2003
Place:	Ohio, USA

ULTIMATE FACTS

A cockatiel is native to the Australian outback, and is also called the Quarrion or Weiro. They are the smallest members of the cockatoo family.

Cockatiels are popular pets. These little birds are colorful, cute, and friendly. With proper care, they also live a long time — around 15 years, in most cases. But one hardy fellow broke into the record books with nearly double that number! Pretty Boy, a cockatiel belonging to Catherine Masarin of Hinckley, Ohio, was more than 28 years old when he qualified officially as the world's **Oldest Cockatiel** on November 3, 2003. Born on September 17, 1975, Pretty Boy lived until the year 2004.

Longest Rabbit

Record-holder:	Amy
Date:	March 23, 2008
Place:	Somerset, UK

ULTIMATE FACTS

Amy comes by her spectacular size naturally. She is a Flemish giant, which is the **Largest Rabbit Breed**. Individuals of this breed regularly weigh 18 pounds or more!

Picture those cute little pet store bunnies you can hold in your cupped hands. Now imagine one of those bunnies growing to the size of a 15-month-old human baby. That's about the size of Amy, the **Longest Rabbit** ever measured! Owned by Annette Edwards of Wookey Hole, Somerset, UK, this robust rabbit measured 2 feet, 8 inches from nose to cotton tail-tip on March 23, 2008 (pictured). Too big to be a house pet, Amy sleeps in her own dog kennel in the backyard. Good thing she doesn't have to dig a burrow. She would need a huge hole to feel at home!

Largest Guinea Pig Litter

Record-holder: Casperina
Date: August 17, 1992
Place: Queensland, Australia

ULTIMATE FACTS

Guinea pig pups are well-developed at birth. They have hair, claws, teeth, and partial eyesight, and they can walk immediately. They can also eat solid food. Because the pups are so independent, they have an excellent chance of survival, even in the largest litters.

Female guinea pigs usually give birth to anywhere between one and six pups per litter. But evidently that wasn't good enough for Casperina, a Guinness World Record-breaking guinea pig owned by Ruth Winkler of Glasshouse Mountains, Queensland, Australia. On August 17, 1992, this mighty mommy produced nine pups — the **Largest Guinea Pig Litter** ever recorded. All of the babies survived, making Casperina not only history's most prolific guinea pig mom, but undoubtedly the busiest, too!

Oldest Goldfish Ever

ULTIMATE FACTS

A group of goldfish is known as a "troubling." It's an odd nickname for such an easygoing pet!

Record-holder:	Tish
Date:	August 1999
Place:	North Yorkshire, UK

In 1956, a boy named Peter Hand won two goldfish at a fair in Doncaster, North Yorkshire. He named his new pets Tish and Tosh. Tosh passed away in 1975, but Tish lived on . . . and on . . . and on. Although he turned from orange to silver as the years went by, Tish was happy and healthy until his death in August 1999. He had reached the grand old age of 43, making him the **Oldest Goldfish Ever** (not pictured). Did a new fish move into Tish's bowl? Of course not. "Tish was part of the family. We couldn't replace him," explained Hilda Hand, Peter's mother.

Longest Domestic Goat Horns

Record-holder:	Uncle Sam
Date:	April 16, 2004
Place:	Pennsylvania, USA

"He had a normal diet and grew up in a normal environment. But the horns just got longer and longer," says Bill Wentling from Rothsville, Pennsylvania, about his record-breaking pet. Bill and Vivian owned Uncle Sam, the goat with the **Longest Domestic Goat Horns**. His pair of twisted horns stretched 52 inches from tip to tip when measured on April 16, 2004 (pictured). That's a whole 10 inches longer than the previous record-holder! Unfortunately, Uncle Sam passed away in 2005. But his Guinness World Record lives on until an even more impressive pair of horns appears!

Tallest Living Horse

Record-holder:	Radar
Date:	July 27, 2004
Place:	Texas, USA

You'll need a stepladder to climb onto the back of a Belgian draft horse named Radar, who holds the Guinness World Record for being the **Tallest Living Horse** (pictured meeting Thumbelina, his record-holding opposite). Radar stood 19 hands 3.5 inches (that's 79.5 inches total) at the shoulder when officially measured at the North American Belgian Championship in London, Ontario, Canada, on July 27, 2004. His owners at Priefert Manufacturing, Inc. in Mount Pleasant, Texas, keep Radar satisfied with a big diet of 40 pounds of hay, 18 pounds of grain, and 20 gallons of water *every day*!

Record-holder:	Thumbelina
Date:	July 7, 2006
Place:	Missouri, USA

ULTIMATE FACTS

For a little horse, Thumbelina sure gets a lot of attention! This chestnut mare has appeared on *The Oprah Winfrey Show*, *The Today Show*, *Good Morning America*, *Live with Regis and Kelly*, and many other TV programs.

Standing just 17.5 inches at the shoulder and "neighing" in at 57 pounds, Thumbelina is by far the **Smallest Living Horse**. Born on May 1, 2001 in St. Louis, Missouri, this pint-sized pony is known as a dwarf miniature or sometimes a "mini-mini." But that doesn't stop Thumbelina from doing a BIG job! Working as a therapy horse, Thumbelina travels far and wide to visit sick, needy, and disabled children. "Thumbelina has become a great inspiration . . . [She] reminds us that everyone has a purpose and that even the least among us can accomplish great things," say owners Kay and Paul Goessling.

Lending a Helping Paw, Hoof, or Wing

🐾 The term "service animal" describes any creature that is specially trained to help a disabled person. Most service animals are dogs. However, many other types of animals, including cats, birds, capuchin monkeys, and miniature horses, have been successfully trained as human helpers.

🐾 The term "therapy animal" (also "comfort animal") describes any creature that is used to comfort people in distress. Therapy animals often visit hospitals, orphanages, retirement homes, and other places where folks need a little pick-me-up.

🐾 Want to help? Almost any friendly, well-behaved pet can serve as a therapy animal. Identify organizations you would like to visit. Contact these organizations to get permission and make appointments. Then show up with your pet to spread a little sunshine!

Visit this book's special color-photo section to see Thumbelina on her therapy tour.

CHAPTER 4

Action Stars

Lights . . . Camera . . . ACTION! These record-breaking pets are always in motion and now you can go with them! Compete in the world's most prestigious dog shows, test your long-jumping skills against Denmark's best hopper, measure your diving heights with a water-loving pig, and traverse a tube with a super-fast ferret. Then you can stop and pose with a canine movie star.

Most Successful International Show Dog

Record-holder: Jucki
Date: November 4, 2001
Place: Iowa, USA

Jucki shows off her trophies in this book's special color-photo section.

ULTIMATE FACTS

German shepherds are also known as Alsatians. They are considered to be the third most intelligent dog breed, behind border collies and poodles.

In 1992, Neal Leas of Redfield, Iowa, traveled to Germany in hopes of discovering the world's next dog-show superstar. He was positive he had found her when he saw Jucki von der Freiheit Westerholt (a.k.a. Jucki), a female German shepherd with incredible potential. Neal paid $17,000 for the dog, and the rest is history. Trained by Neal's daughter, Holly Anne, Jucki proceeded to take Best in Show honors in 67 championships on five continents during a period of nine years (1992-2001). This remarkable record qualifies Jucki as the **Most Successful International Show Dog** of all time.

More Top Dogs

So your dog doesn't have a perfect pedigree, coat, or attitude. That's okay. There are plenty of competitions for the average pup, including these:

World's Ugliest Dog Competition — The famous contest happens every year at the Sonoma-Marin Fair in Petaluma, California. The record-holder for **Ugliest Dog** is Chi Chi, a rare African sand dog with 7 wins. His grandson Rascal, a hairless Chinese Crested owned by Dane Andrew of Sunnyvale, California, has won these "beauty" contests since 2002 (pictured).

U.S. Disc Dog Nationals — In this annual event, dogs show off their flying disc catching abilities. Fancy footwork and flips earn extra points!

Dock Jumping Competitions — These events allow water-loving dogs to show off their long-jumping skills. Pooches of all shapes and sizes catapult themselves off docks in hopes of capturing the distance prize!

▲ World's Ugliest
Dog Competition

◀ Dock Jumping
Competitions

Longest Jump by a Rabbit

Record-holder:	Yabo
Date:	June 12, 1999
Place:	Horsens, Denmark

Former champion Golden Flame displays her jumping skills in this book's special color-photo section.

ULTIMATE FACTS

Kaninhop originated in Sweden in the late 1970s. Today, there are more than 50 rabbit-hopping clubs across Scandinavia.

"Rabbit hopping," or *kaninhop*, is a popular sport in many Scandinavian countries. At *kaninhop* competitions, cotton-tailed athletes bound over and across various obstacles. The bounciest bunnies win trophies and, sometimes, a Guinness World Record! One such title was earned in Horsens, Denmark, on June 12, 1999. A rabbit named Yabo leaped a distance of 9 feet, 9.6 inches — the **Longest Jump by a Rabbit**. Yabo was guided by his owner, Maria Bruun Jensen, who used a light leash to lead her pet to the course's start.

Highest Jump by a Guinea Pig

Record-holder:	Puckel Martin
Date:	March 16, 2003
Place:	Vargön, Sweden

ULTIMATE FACTS

Guinea pigs have natural jumping abilities. They tend to leap around whenever they feel happy and excited. This behavior is called "popcorning" or "pronking."

Guinea pigs are small, cute, cuddly . . . and able to leap tall objects in a single bound! Puckel Martin is the rotund record-holder for **Highest Jump by a Guinea Pig** (not pictured). Owned by Madde Herrman of Vargön, Sweden, Puckel hurdled an obstacle towering 7.8 inches above surface level on March 16, 2003. The star athlete later proved his jumping power during the *Ultimate Guinness World Records* TV show, which originally aired in the UK in 2006.

Longest Dive by a Pig

Record-holder:	Miss Piggy
Date:	July 22, 2005
Place:	Northern Territory, Australia

The phrase "when pigs fly" means that something will *never* happen. But on July 22, 2005, it did happen when a five-month-old porker named Miss Piggy zoomed through the air with the greatest of ease (not pictured)! The high-flying feat took place for the *Guinness World Records* TV show. Miss Piggy trotted up a ramp onto a diving board, then leaped 10 feet, 10 inches into a pool at the Royal Darwin Show in Australia's Northern Territory. How was the swine's splashdown greeted? With the record for **Longest Dive by a Pig** and *squeals* of joy from the crowd!

Miss Piggy's owner, Tom Vandeleur, is convinced that all pigs are good divers. "Pigs are water animals. They love the water. They've got no fear of it. It's just the height problem they have to overcome," he says.

These piglet competitors swim for a medal at the "Pig Olympics" held in Shanghai, China.

Fastest Ferret

Record-holder:	Warhol
Date:	July 11, 1999
Place:	Northumberland, UK

Ferrets excel at squeezing through narrow passages. Racing ferrets through a series of tubes is a competitive sport in some countries. On July 11, 1999, an albino ferret named Warhol beat 150 competitors to win the World Ferret Racing Championship in Blyth, Northumberland. He earned his trophy (pictured), along with the Guinness World Record as **Fastest Ferret**, by zipping through 32 feet, 9 inches of plastic tubing in just 12.59 seconds. "Warhol obviously decided this was his big moment and really went for it," said race organizer Jane Bewlay. The newspapers nicknamed him "Berwickshire's White Lightning." But to owner Jacqui Adams, the fleet-footed superstar was simply Warhol, her treasured 18-month-old pet.

Most Skips by a Dog in One Minute

Record-holder:	Swee'pea
Date:	August 8, 2007
Place:	New York, USA

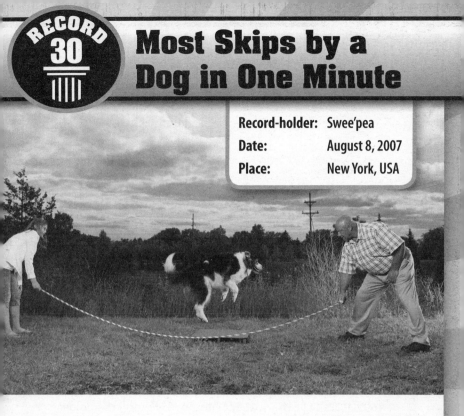

It takes a lot of courage to attempt setting a Guinness World Record on live TV. But the pressure didn't bother Swee'pea, an Australian shepherd/border collie cross who stole the show during "Guinness World Record Breakers Week" on US talk program *Live with Regis and Kelly* filmed in New York City on August 8, 2007. Owner and trainer Alex "Popeye" Rothacker swung a rope while Swee'pea jumped it 75 times in a single minute, keeping her title for **Most Skips by a Dog in One Minute**. Swee'pea had set two previous records in this category, first with 62 skips and later with 65. She can jump the rope alone or with friends (pictured). Stick around because Alex and his star student aren't done wowing you with their doggone tricks!

Most Steps Walked Up by a Dog Facing Forward Balancing a Glass of Water

Record-holder:	Swee'pea
Date:	August 8, 2007
Place:	New York, USA

See Swee'pea's balancing act in this book's special color-photo section.

ULTIMATE FACTS

Anyone can take dog-training lessons at the Tops Kennel Complex in Grayslake, Illinois, home of Alex and Swee'pea. Maybe your pup could learn to be the next Guinness World Records champion!

Thought we were done with Swee'pea? This dog is a dual record-holder, a tough challenge to master, but she makes it look like fun! On the same record-setting day of August 8, 2007, the deft dog ascended 17 stairs while carrying a glass of water on her snout. That's the **Most Steps Walked Up by a Dog Facing Forward Balancing a Glass of Water**. Will she ever top her current records? Probably not. Luckily for the other rope-skipping and balancing canine hopefuls, Swee'pea retired in 2009, leaving the field — or, in this case, the stage — wide open.

Earliest Canine Film Star

Record-holder:	Rollie Rover
Date:	1907
Place:	UK

ULTIMATE FACTS

Rescued by Rover cost less than $40 to make the entire film! With such low production costs, the action-pup movie is one of the cheapest commercial films ever created.

The first commercial motion pictures were shown in 1895. After that, it was only 12 years before the first movie starring a dog took over theaters! *Rescued by Rover*, a black-and-white film released in 1907 in the UK, featured a pooch named Rollie Rover who saved the day by finding a kidnapped baby. Rover quickly catapulted to fame, becoming the **Earliest Canine Film Star**. He was so popular, that his film's negative wore out from being copied over and over and over. Producer Cecil Hepworth ended up reshooting the film — twice — to keep Rover's heroics in the public eye.

Balto

Hotel for Dogs

Box-Office Bowzers

Rollie Rover may have been the first movie-star mutt, but he was far from the last. Rover was quickly followed by Jean, a border collie who starred in the 1910 feature *Jean and the Calico Doll* and several subsequent movies. Then came Rin Tin Tin, Lassie, Benji, and many others. The "pups on film" trend continues today with hit movies such as *Beverly Hills Chihuahua*, *Marley & Me*, *Hotel for Dogs*, and even animated features such as *Balto* and *Bolt* taking a bite out of the box office. In our homes and in our theaters, we sure do love our dogs!

Marley & Me

Lassie

CHAPTER 5

Courageous Companions

Most pets give love and affection to their human owners. The records in this chapter show how some pets give even more. You're about to meet an entire roster of courageous animal companions, including a life-saving parrot, a pint-sized police pup, and a service dog that not only fetches his owner's wash but folds it, too. It's all in a day's work for these furry and feathered friends, who are winners every single day!

Most Lives Saved by a Parrot

Record-holder:	Charlie
Date:	December 1999
Place:	Durham, UK

ULTIMATE FACTS

Patricia Tunnicliffe suffered second-degree burns while escaping from her blazing residence. "Charlie saved our lives," she said later of her beloved pet.

It's a good thing for the Tunnicliffe family of Durham, UK, that their pet parrot, Charlie, knew how to squawk the word "help." In December 1999, Charlie's alarmed, middle-of-the-night cries woke mom Patricia, who discovered that her house was on fire. Patricia ushered her five children to safety. Sadly, smoke from a fire is also dangerous, and Charlie didn't survive. Thanks to his heroic actions, Charlie is credited with rescuing six people from almost certain death — the **Most Lives Saved by a Parrot**.

Most Celebrated Canine Rescuer

Record-holder:	Barry
Date:	Early 1800s
Place:	Swiss Alps

ULTIMATE FACTS

Barry's most famous rescue involved a boy buried by an avalanche. Barry used his thick furry body to keep the boy warm until he awoke, then he carried the boy upon his back to safety!

Throughout history, dogs have been known to help people out of dangerous situations. But when it comes to heroism, one dog stands head and tail above the rest! Living in a monastery along the storm-swept Swiss/Italian border, Barry the Saint Bernard served as a rescue dog between 1800 and 1812. During this time, Barry found and saved at least 40 travelers, making him the **Most Celebrated Canine Rescuer** of all time. Today, a monument has been erected in Barry's honor. It stands guard at the entrance of a famous pet cemetery in Paris, France.

Smallest Police Dog

Record-holder: Midge
Date: November 7, 2006
Place: Ohio, USA

Flip to this book's special color-photo section for Midge's patriotic portrait.

ULTIMATE FACTS

Midge is certified by the state of Ohio as a narcotics dog. This means she is qualified to do sensitive searches, and her actions are recognized by courts and judges during trials.

You don't have to be big to be tough! A petite pup named Midge proves this fact every day in her work as an official Law Enforcement Work Dog (or "Police K9") for the Geauga County Sheriff's Office in Chardon, Ohio. Measuring a tiny 11 inches tall and 23 inches long, this Chihuahua/rat terrier mix is the world's **Smallest Police Dog**. Midge accompanies her owner, Sheriff Dan McClelland, wherever he goes. She swings into action during arrests, property searches, and drug-seizure operations, using her small but highly trained nose to sniff out drugs.

Super Sniffers

Midge's accomplishments are impressive. It will be a while, though, before she can challenge the record of Trepp, the golden retriever who holds the Guinness World Record as the **Most Successful Police Dog.** Trepp (which is short for "Intrepid") has been credited with more than 100 arrests and the recovery of more than $63 million worth of narcotics. While on the subject of super sniffers, we must mention Snag, a Labrador retriever who works for US Customs. He has helped officers make 118 drug seizures worth $810 million and earned the title of **Most Successful Sniffer Dog** (not pictured). Ah, the sweet *smell* of success!

Highest-Ranking Law-Enforcement Camel

Record-holder: Bert
Date: April 5, 2003
Place: California, USA

Get an up-close look at Bert in this book's special color-photo section.

ULTIMATE FACTS

The L.A. County Sheriff's Department employs many animals. Dogs, goats, horses, bison, birds, snakes, and even spiders are part of the county's law-enforcement team.

Every day, Bert the camel goes to work with his handler, Nance Fite. But he's not tagging along. As a Reserve Deputy Sheriff for the Los Angeles County Sheriff's Department in San Dimas, California, Bert is a *real* police camel. In fact, he is the world's **Highest-Ranking Law-Enforcement Camel**! Deputized on April 5, 2003, Bert wears an L.A. County Sheriff's ID around his neck and a badge on his harness. He and Nancy reinforce safety and anti-drug messages at community events and parades. "The kids just flock to him," says a coworker. "He's our number-one crowd pleaser."

Most Guide Dogs Trained by an Organization

Record-holder:	Guide Dogs for the Blind Association
Date:	2006
Place:	Berkshire, UK

ULTIMATE FACTS

Labrador/golden retriever mixes make great guide dogs. Other commonly chosen breeds include German shepherds, poodles, collies, and Labradoodles (Labrador/poodle mix).

Dogs are called man's best friend. For the vision-impaired, guide dogs truly are man's (or woman's) most reliable set of eyes. These working dogs lead their owners safely around obstacles and across streets. It's not surprising that these carefully trained animals are in high demand. The Guide Dogs for the Blind Association of Berkshire, UK, is there to meet the need! As of 2006, GDBA had successfully trained 26,019 dogs — the **Most Guide Dogs Trained by an Organization**. Funded completely by donations, the organization has 1,000 employees and more than 10,000 volunteers. That's a whole lot of people doing a whole lot of good!

75 Years of Success

The Guide Dogs for the Blind Association was founded in 1934. Operating out of a garage in Cheshire, UK, the fledgling business could train only a few dogs at a time. Today, GDBA has grown into a huge operation with four training centers across the UK. The organization breeds about 1,000 puppies a year but admits only the best, smartest, and friendliest of these pups into its training program. The "washouts" sometimes go on to careers with different assistance-dog organizations, such as Hearing Dogs for Deaf People or Dogs for the Disabled. Others find love and happiness as treasured family pets.

Most Clothes Retrieved from a Washing Line by a Dog in One Minute

Record-holder:	Vesta
Date:	April 2, 2009
Place:	London, UK

Guide dogs don't *only* help vision-impaired people. They can be trained to aid all types of disabled people with everyday chores. Dan Smith is wheelchair-bound, and his companion animal is a Labrador named Vesta (pictured). Labradors are bred to be excellent retrievers. They love to play "fetch" with their owners and to collect things in every way imaginable. Vesta received special training from Dogs for the Disabled (UK) to improve the quality of Dan's life by assisting him in specific daily tasks, such as doing laundry. Vesta displayed her fetch-and-fold skills on the set of the TV show, *Guinness World Records: Smashed,* in London, UK. On April 2, 2009, she took less than 60 seconds to grab eight hung-up towels and place them in a basket. That's the record for **Most Clothes Retrieved from a Washing Line by a Dog in One Minute**!

CHAPTER 6

Friends Through Time

After reading the previous five chapters, you might think the world has gone pet-crazy in recent years. But you'd be wrong, and Guinness World Records has the evidence to prove it! From the oldest civilizations to present day, people have always cherished animals as their friends and helpers. Read on to learn about mankind's millennia-long devotion to dogs, cats, tortoises, and . . . elephants? This is the grand finish to our pet lovers' parade!

Oldest Chelonian

Record-holder:	Tu'i Malila
Date:	May 19, 1965
Place:	Tonga

Most animals brighten their owner's lives for a short time before moving on to pet paradise. But a tortoise named Tu'i Malila received such royal treatment through 18 generations of owners that he lived on to earn the title of **Oldest Chelonian**! The chelonian group includes all tortoises, turtles, and terrapins. This Madagascar radiated tortoise was given to the royal family of Tonga as a gift by famed explorer James Cook, around the year 1777 (pictured). Tu'i Malila remained in his original family's care until he died of natural causes on May 19, 1965, at the grand old age of 188 years.

Oldest Dog Breed

Record-holder:	Saluki
Date:	329 BCE
Place:	Ancient Egypt

The American Kennel Club (AKC) recognizes 157 dog breeds. Some of these breeds have emerged in recent decades. Others have been around for thousands of years. The "granddaddy" of the AKC list is the Saluki (pictured), which is believed to have emerged in 329 BCE. This early arrival makes the Saluki the **Oldest Dog Breed** ever recorded. Salukis were especially revered in ancient Egypt, where they were kept as royal pets. They were even mummified after death so they could go with their owners on their journey into the afterlife. Now *that's* a faithful friend!

Earliest Domesticated Cat

Record-holder:	Shillourokambos skeleton
Date:	7,500 BCE
Place:	Cyprus

ULTIMATE FACTS

The Shillourokambos skeleton is large and built more like an African wildcat than a present-day domestic cat. It represents an extremely early stage in the human/cat relationship.

Dogs weren't the only animals adored by long-ago humans. Archaeological findings prove that cats have been living with people for thousands of years. The oldest known evidence of cat domestication was discovered in 2004 in the Stone-Age village of Shillourokambos on Cyprus. Here, scientists uncovered the 9,500-year-old bones of a human and a cat that seem to have been buried together. If this is the case, the feline fossil is the remains of the **Earliest Domesticated Cat**. What a PURR-fect discovery!

First Domesticated Elephants

Record-holder:	Asian elephant
Date:	2,000 BCE
Place:	Present-day Pakistan and India

Unlike cats and dogs, early elephants were not kept as pets. They were, however, tamed and used as farm animals, war mounts, royal "vehicles," and much more. The **First Domesticated Elephants** probably made their appearance around 2,000 BCE during the Indus Valley civilization in the region of present-day Pakistan and India. Asian elephants were mostly used as beasts of burden. Larger, more aggressive African elephants were chosen for military purposes. Today, elephants don't do much fighting, but they are still put to work (pictured). An estimated 3,400 of these animals still live on farms and in logging camps throughout modern-day India.

Most working elephants are female — for good reason. Male elephants are bigger and harder to handle. Sometimes the males enter a state called *musth*, during which hormonal changes make them angry and aggressive.

Domestic Bliss?

The earliest peoples hunted for food or simply gathered whatever they could find. But about 12,000 years ago, certain groups became farmers. They planted their own crops. They also established herds of goats, sheep, cattle, and pigs — the first domesticated animals on Earth. Since that time, humans have domesticated hundreds of species as working animals, food sources, or companions.

By definition, domestic animals are those that have been bred in captivity for a long time. Their territories, food supply, and other opportunities are controlled by humans. Therefore, elephants are not truly domesticated. Most working elephants were born in the wild. They have been captured, tamed, and trained to do specific jobs.

Record-holder:	Australia
Date:	2003

ULTIMATE FACTS

According to the American Veterinary Medicine Association, 57.4 percent of all U.S. households contained at least one pet in 2007.

Blimey, mate! Down under, they sure do think their pets are *bonzer*! According to statistics compiled by the Australian Companion Animal Council, Australia had the **Highest Rate of Pet Ownership** of any nation as of 2003. An estimated 66 percent of households owned at least one animal as a companion, and 83 percent of Australians had owned a pet at some point in their life. The 2003 tally of 38 million animals included nearly 2.5 million cats, 3.75 million dogs, 9 million birds, and a staggering 20 million fish. Hamsters, ferrets, rabbits, reptiles, and many other critters made up the rest of the pet parade, which more than qualified for a Guinness World Record!

Largest Pet Store

Record-holder:	Zoo Zajac
Date:	September 2005
Place:	Duisburg, Germany

ULTIMATE FACTS

An average US pet super-store covers an area of about 19,000 square feet. That's less than one-fourth the size of the incredible Zoo Zajac.

A football field covers an area of 57,600 square feet. That's about *two-thirds* the size of Zoo Zajac, the super-sized shop that holds the Guinness World Record as the **Largest Pet Store** anywhere! Owned and managed by Norbert Zajac of Duisburg, Germany, the incredible emporium covered an area of 86,867.21 feet when it was measured in September 2005. Zoo Zajac's website claims that more than 4 million people have strolled the store's aisles since its grand opening in November 2004. It's a good thing there was plenty of elbow room for all those shoppers!

Record-holder:	Barkingham Palace
Date:	Fall 2008
Place:	Gloucestershire, UK

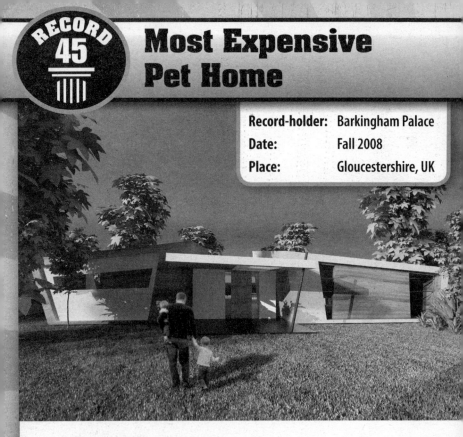

The press has dubbed it "Barkingham Palace," and it's easy to see why. Commissioned in 2008, the **Most Expensive Pet Home** on record will cost an estimated $384,623 when complete. Its two Great Dane residents will live in the "yap" of luxury with a 52-inch plasma TV, temperature-controlled beds, a doggie spa, automatic dispensers for filtered water and deluxe dry food, a private playground, and many other grand features (pictured). Designed by architect Andy Ramus and located in the fancy Lower Mill Estate near Cirencester, Gloucestershire, the deluxe doghouse will be a quarter the size of the human house upon the same lot. That's quite a kennel!

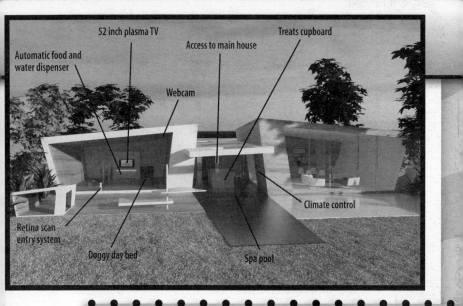

Automatic food and water dispenser

52 inch plasma TV

Webcam

Access to main house

Treats cupboard

Climate control

Retina scan entry system

Doggy day bed

Spa pool

Barkingham Palace

The deluxe doghouse will also feature these amenities:

- 🐾 Retina-controlled dog flaps
- 🐾 Climate control
- 🐾 Two private bedrooms and a day lounge
- 🐾 A state-of-the-art sound system
- 🐾 Self-cleaning eating and drinking bowls
- 🐾 Webcams to allow owner monitoring
- 🐾 An outdoor lounge with additional TV

Largest Gathering of Pets

Record-holder:	Feria de las Flores
Date:	August 7, 2007
Place:	Medellín, Colombia

ULTIMATE FACTS

The Feria de las Flores has been the scene of another Guinness World Records triumph. The festival holds the title for **Largest Outdoor Horse Parade** with more than 7,000 horses and riders on the march on July 29, 2006.

The annual Feria de las Flores (Festival of the Flowers) is the biggest and best-loved event of the year in Medellín, Colombia. So perhaps it is appropriate that Medellín residents chose this venue to celebrate their *big* affection for their *best-loved* animal companions! On August 7, 2007, thousands of proud pet owners took 4,616 animal friends for a group stroll during the flower festival, earning the Guinness World Record for **Largest Gathering of Pets** in the process. Pretty *blooming* impressive, if you ask us!

CONCLUSION

STAY A LITTLE LONGER

Our parade has wrapped up, but your visit with record-setting pets doesn't have to stop here. Meet more of the world's animal companions in the online archives (*www.guinnessworldrecords.com*) and within the pages of *Guinness World Records* at your local library or bookstore. You're guaranteed to find thousands of records covering all things big, small, long, short, least, most, and many other sensational superlatives.

Interested in making history by having your own record? Check out the official guidelines featured on the next page on how you — or your pet — can become a record-breaker. Maybe your name will appear in the next edition of the record books!

Message from the Keeper of the Records:

Record-breakers are the ultimate in one way or another — the youngest, the oldest, the tallest, the smallest. So how do you get to be a record-breaker? Follow these important steps:

1. Before you attempt your record, check with us to make sure your record is suitable and safe. Get your parents' permission. Next, contact one of our officials by using the record application form at *www.guinnessworldrecords.com.*

2. Tell us about your idea. Give us as much information as you can, including what the record is, when you want to attempt it, where you'll be doing it, and other relevant information.

a) We will tell you if a record already exists, what safety guidelines you must follow during your attempt to break that record, and what evidence we need as proof that you completed your attempt.

b) If your idea is a brand-new record nobody has set yet, we need to make sure it meets our requirements. If it does, then we'll write official rules and safety guidelines specific to that record idea and make sure all attempts are made in the same way.

3. Whether it is a new or existing record, we will send you the guidelines for your selected record. Once you receive these, you can make your attempt at any time. You do not need a Guinness World Record official at your attempt. But you do need to gather evidence. Find out more about the kind of evidence we need to see by visiting our website.

4. Think you've already set or broken a record? Put all of your evidence as specified by the guidelines in an envelope and mail it to us at Guinness World Records.

5. Our officials will investigate your claim fully — a process that can take a few weeks, depending on the number of claims we've received and how complex your record is.

6. If you're successful, you will receive an official certificate that says you are now a Guinness World Record-holder!

Need more info? Check out *www.guinnessworldrecords.com* for lots more hints, tips, and some top record ideas. Good luck!

PHOTO CREDITS

The publisher would like to thank the following for their kind permission to use their photographs in this book: